Dear Reader,

Some tales at once excite you,

Some tales told twice are true.

Come with me. I invite you

Along for the derring-do—

To a tale as keen as a cutlass

That no man dares impeach.

A tale to billow a pirate's sail

Is the tale of Captain Teach.

Blackbeard
The Pirate King

SEVERAL YARNS DETAILING
THE LEGENDS, MYTHS,
AND REAL-LIFE ADVENTURES
OF HISTORY'S MOST
NOTORIOUS SEAMAN
TOLD IN VERSE BY
J. PATRICK LEWIS

NATIONAL GEOGRAPHIC
WASHINGTON, D.C.

The Brethren of the Coast

Golden Age of Piracy   1698 – 1730

Down Caribbean shipping lanes,
Where buccaneers held court,
The pistol, blade,
And cannon made
Their treachery blood sport.

"The Brethren of the Coast," pirates
No country could contain,
Loved stealing gold
And seas patrolled—
To a man they hated Spain.

But of all the thieves of the Seven Seas,
No one would ever reach
The height and might
Of the roguish Knight
Of the Black Flag, Edward Teach.

The Treaty of Utrecht (1712) *brought an end to Queen Anne's War, or the War of the Spanish Succession, leaving thousands of seamen freed from military service and without jobs. Many turned to the pirate trade, where each captain's Articles of Agreement (an agreement signed by each seaman as he joined a crew) set rules for conduct, the sharing of plunder (stolen goods), and shipboard elections.*

—

RIGHT: "DUEL ON THE BEACH," BY N. C. WYETH, 1926

Apprentice Pirate

Well-spent Fortune ✦ *Misspent Youth*

Born in 1680
(No one can say for sure),
Possibly in Bristol, England,
Early life, obscure,
Teach heard them calling longingly—
The sirens of the sea.
Obsessed, he navigated west.
His landfall? Destiny.

Sometime between 1702 and 1713,
Was it a Jamaica privateer
That sailed for the Queen?
And did Teach prove his valor
And his boldness to the cause
Of Queen Anne's War before he set
About to breaking laws?

Apprenticed to the famous pirate
Benjamin Hornigold,
Teach taught the crew a thing or two,
And the future was foretold.
New Providence, Bahamas,
Was this sea dog's port of call.
He would become the most
Swashbuckling buccaneer of all.

—

The Queen Anne's Revenge

Latter part of 1717   *St. Vincent, West Indies*

The slaves-for-cargo *Concorde,*
    Flying the flag of France,
Took broadsides and surrendered
    At the pirates' quick advance.
The capture of that prize ship
    Was Blackbeard's rich reward,
Three hundred men and forty cannon
    Outfitted aboard.

Newly named *Queen Anne's Revenge,*
    The ship was rigged to please
Blackbeard in weather fair or foul
    And inhospitable seas.
And who could say what horrified
    Those hunted ships the more—
The specter of *Revenge* or
    Its bearded commodore?

Blackbeard attacked Concorde, *a 250-ton French merchant ship, from two sloops.*

He had commandeered the larger one, the 60-ton Revenge, *from fellow pirate Stede Bonnet. Following the battle,*

he gave the smaller, 40-ton sloop to the French captain and crew, who renamed her Mauvaise Rencontre *(Bad*

Encounter) and sailed her and their remaining human cargo to Martinique, where they recorded their misadventure.

—

THESE PAGES: STRIKING THE COLORS OF *CONCORDE,* BY GARY KELLEY, 2005

Edward Teach as Blackbeard

Witness to Wonder ❧ *Larger than Life*

Now Teach was as tall as a waterfall

And strong as a rum-soaked cask.

The sea would quake in the sloop's wide wake

When he took a man to task,

For what men feared was the coal-black beard

Some said was the devil's mask.

His beard began beneath his eyes,

Curled down in pigtail braids,

Festooned with colored ribbons that

Ensured the renegade's

First step to a reputation

For amazing escapades.

No seaman soon forgot the sneer

For which he was well known—

Or cannon fuses lit under

His hat! His visage shown

So frightful that it chilled his foes

Straight to the marrowbone.

The only eyewitness account we have of Blackbeard reads:

"The Captain was a tall Spare Man with a very black beard which he wore very long."

Did the name Blackbeard come from this description? No one knows. The bearded legend's real name may have been Teach

or Thatch or Tach, but we do know that it was in his lifetime that he became known as Blackbeard.

—

LEFT: ONE OF THE EARLIEST KNOWN IMAGES OF BLACKBEARD, BY THOMAS NICHOLLS, c. 1730

A Pirate's Colors

Though often running up a flag
    Meant mercy would be shown,
For some a pirate's colors cried,
    Leave well enough alone.

Now a famous Jolly Roger that
    Could capture Blackbeard's art
Was the skull-and-crossbones death's head
    That could stop a human heart.

But what's a rumor worth at sea
    That passes for suspense?
Of scores of men they say he killed,
    There is no evidence.

Flags were certainly part of the romantic etiquette of the Golden Age of Pirates. Flags, often called "colors," were a calling card at sea. Blackbeard's flag is commonly thought to be the one shown in this painting, although historic documents indicate that he probably flew the traditional skull-and-crossbones.

———

THESE PAGES: "BLACKBEARD AFIRE," BY RICK FARRELL, 2000

In the Wake of the Sloops

From the Carolinas   *To the Bahamas*

In 1717 Blackbeard fled
New Providence. Before
He reached America, he struck
Like "a frightening meteor."
The *Betty* of Virginia,
The *Robert,* and the *Good*
Intent just out of Dublin—
Oh, he plundered all he could,
Relieving them of cargo,
Spices, silverware, and gold,
Bay rum, Madeira wine, and then
He stowed it in the hold.

Pirates frequently faced vessels at sea that were bigger than their own, like the Spanish galleon seen in this painting. Merchant ships were often ill-prepared and ill-equipped to combat the cannon power of a well-fitted pirate ship or sloop.

Pirates used guile and cunning as much as boldness to overpower their enemies.

They were not above lying low to imitate an abandoned ship or dressing up like women on deck to lure the merchantmen and their precious cargo into their treacherous hands.

RIGHT: "AN ATTACK ON A GALLEON," BY HOWARD PYLE, 1905

Blackbeard at Play

Astonishing Adventures 🌟 *Fantastic Escapades*

Carousing in the taverns
With his Nassau *bons amis*,
Teach bragged with the same gusto
He attacked vessels at sea.

Once he mixed black gunpowder
In a glass of island rum.
When it caught fire, he guzzled it!
Onlookers were struck dumb.

Blackbeard enjoyed a good game.

Large sailing vessels often carried a supply of sulfur pots that were routinely used to smoke out insects and rodents. It has been said that Blackbeard would light several of these pots of sulfur, close the hatches, and challenge his men to see who could stay below deck the longest. Fact or fiction, it's a great yarn.

—

LEFT: "BLACKBEARD IN SMOKE AND FLAMES," BY FRANK EARLE SCHOONOVER, 1922
ABOVE: "BLACKBEARD ON ISLAND," BY H. CHARLES MCBARRON, EARLY 1960s

Blackbeard Gives a Lesson

The First Mate   *Learns His Fate*

One night he sat there drinking
With his first mate, Israel Hands,
And shot him in the knee, and said,
"Just so's you understands,

"No man should take a notion
That a Captain's place is his.
A running dog, you dog,
Should not forget just who he is."

We do not know if this story is true. We do know that after Blackbeard's death, Israel Hands testified against his fellow crewmates and avoided the gallows.

—

THESE PAGES: BLACKBEARD SHOOTS ISRAEL HANDS, BY FRANK EARLE SCHOONOVER, 1922

The Blockade of Charleston

A Feat of Daring ❧ A Show of Strength

'Twas a blockade bold and daring,

A great escapade declaring

Blackbeard Pirate King supreme.

Sleepy Charleston was shaken,

Several hostages were taken

For the purpose of his scheme.

Not a single gun was fired.

All that Blackbeard had required

Were some medical supplies.

One would think that he'd demand some

Money, gold, and jewels as ransom,

But one has to realize,

Though the town was far from quiet,

He'd avoided any riot

And pursued his livelihood.

Blackbeard humbled—his ambition—

Charleston into submission

Just to prove a pirate could.

*Six months before Blackbeard's rule over the Atlantic coast came to a grisly end,
the Blockade of Charleston was perhaps his finest hour. In stopping all inbound and outbound vessels, he engaged in
his most brazen act of piracy by humiliating the port city without firing a single shot. Throughout his career of piracy,
there is no evidence that Blackbeard ever killed anyone, apart from during the final battle at Ocracoke.*

—

LEFT: BLACKBEARD APPROACHES, BY FRANK EARLE SCHOONOVER, 1922

Piracy Runs Aground

June 1718   ✤   *Beaufort Inlet*

A week beyond the Charleston blockade,
The crafty Edward Teach devised a stunning
Deception worthy of a king of cunning.
He and a few trustworthy mates betrayed
So many hearties who'd been Blackbeard-true.
In what appeared an accident, he planned
To run his famous flagship on the sand.
Until shock of his intrigue, no one knew
He'd steal away with all the jewels and gold.
Later, he hoped to wrangle a King's pardon
For piracy. But adversaries harden—
Things fall apart, the center does not hold.
Months later, he would leave one thought behind:
The Pirate King, swashbuckling in our mind.

After Blackbeard's spectacular betrayal of his own seamen, he set sail aboard the Spanish sloop that he had captured a few months earlier near Cuba. He sailed his newly named Adventure, laden with riches, north toward Bath, North Carolina, where he accepted a King's pardon for his piracy.

—

THESE PAGES: QUEEN ANNE'S REVENGE AGROUND, BY RICHARD SCHLECHT, 1999

The Battle of Ocracoke Inlet

November 22, 1718   *Pamlico Sound, North Carolina*

I

Attack! The warnings were in vain.

Teach lay at anchor and at ease.

But lurking at the point, the *Jane,*

A 35-man sloop would seize

The moment when, feigning defeat,

It drifted closer. Half its crew

Jumped from the hold prepared to meet

Blackbeard—a fateful rendezvous!

"If we should fall to lesser foe

Like Captain Maynard's men," he swore,

"Then Caesar, light the powder, blow

The ship and them to nevermore!"

But Caesar, Blackbeard's loyal mate,

An African, frightfully large,

Was stopped before it was too late.

He never carried out the charge.

Blackbeard may have taken brief retirement from pirating following his King's pardon.

We know that he married during this time, but by September of 1718, there is evidence

that he was back in command as the Pirate King.

—

LEFT: "EXPECT NO QUARTER," BY RICK REEVES, 1998

II

Oh they rushed him and they grabbed him,
And they shot him and they stabbed him
With five pistol balls and twenty slashing swords.
To the end he did not tender
One despicable surrender,
As he staggered, bloody, lifeless, to the boards.

Just before dawn, Lieutenant Maynard's two sloops weighed anchor outside Ocracoke Inlet and headed to what has become known as Teach's Hole. Eyewitnesses reported that Blackbeard and Maynard shouted curses at one another and that the two men swore not to "give or take quarter" (no surrender, a fight to the death). Blackbeard broadsided both of Maynard's vessels, disabling Ranger and apparently disabling Jane. Thinking he had won, the Pirate King and his men boarded Jane, not knowing Maynard's men lay in wait. The end came quickly.

—

LEFT: "THE CAPTURE OF THE PIRATE BLACKBEARD," BY JEAN LEON GEROME FERRIS, 1921
ABOVE: BLACKBEARD IS SLAIN BY LT. ROBERT MAYNARD, BY GEORGE VARIAN, c. 1897

At Teach's Hole

Death Sails 🦋 *By Moonlight*

The ghostly headless figure
Of Blackbeard, it is said,
Still swims under the moonlight
Looking for its severed head.

But who knows where the truth lies
In tales of derring-do.
The tales that most excite you
Are the tales twice told and true.

LEFT: SEA PIECE BY MOONLIGHT, BY CASPAR DAVID FRIEDRICH, 1835
ABOVE: BLACKBEARD'S HEAD ON THE END OF THE BOWSPRIT, ARTIST UNKNOWN, c. 1837

Blackbeard's Last Voyage

Albemarle Sound

Pamlico Sound

Cape Hatteras

Ocracoke Inlet
(Teach's Hole)

Site of
Blackbeard's death
(November 1718)

Bath

NORTH CAROLINA

Wreck of the
Queen Anne's Revenge
(June 1718)

Beaufort Inlet
(Old Top Sail Inlet)

Cape
Lookout

Atlantic Ocean

Wilmington

Cape
Fear
River

Stede Bonnet's
Capture

Cape
Fear

SOUTH CAROLINA

Charleston

Blackbeard's
Blockade (May 1718)

miles

0   10   20   30   40   50

Present-day boundaries and shorelines are shown.

A NOTE FROM THE AUTHOR

If oceans could speak, what deep secrets the Atlantic would tell of grand voyages of discovery, famous naval battles, the last desperate hours of sea-tossed sailors, and not least, the age of piracy, cutlass, and cannon, when villainy ruled the waves.

Much of what little we know of Blackbeard's life and times is found in Captain Charles Johnson's *A General History of the Pyrates,* first published in 1724, just a few years after Blackbeard's death. There are primary source documents such as newspaper articles, depositions, and other records that help us fill in his story. For example, merchant shipping records and legal documents tell us of at least 50 ships and sloops, one turtler (a small turtle-hunting boat), and one periauger (a large dugout canoe frequently used to navigate inland waters) that Blackbeard attacked between September 1717 and September 1718. But over the years, facts have mingled with hearsay and embellishment and the imagination of writers and illustrators whose collective voice has given us a charismatic and mythic portrait of the Pirate King.

It is almost a certainty that a particular shipwreck discovered at Beaufort Inlet in 1996 is the pirate's flagship, *Queen Anne's Revenge.* Still, the mystery of Blackbeard lies not at the bottom of a shallow bay but deep in the mind of anyone who muses on the Pirate King.

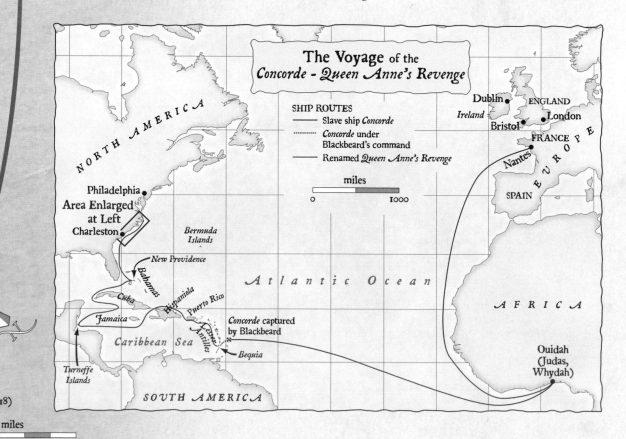

The Voyage of the Concorde - Queen Anne's Revenge

SHIP ROUTES
— Slave ship *Concorde*
···· *Concorde* under Blackbeard's command
— Renamed *Queen Anne's Revenge*

miles

0   1000

NORTH AMERICA

Philadelphia

Area Enlarged at Left

Charleston

Bermuda Islands

New Providence

Bahamas

Cuba

Hispaniola

Puerto Rico

Jamaica

Lesser Antilles

Concorde captured by Blackbeard

Bequia

Turneffe Islands

Caribbean Sea

SOUTH AMERICA

Atlantic Ocean

Dublin   ENGLAND
Ireland   London
        Bristol
    FRANCE
    Nantes
        EUROPE
    SPAIN

AFRICA

Ouidah
(Judas, Whydah)

BLACKBEARD'S TIME LINE

c. 1680 Edward Teach Is Born, Probably in Bristol, England.
Teach's birthplace could also have been London, Jamaica, or even Philadelphia, Pennsylvania.

1702– Queen Anne's War.
1713 Blackbeard possibly operated out of Jamaica as a privateer during Queen Anne's War, turning to piracy after the War.

1713 Blackbeard After the War.
Blackbeard may have served as a crewman aboard a Jamaican sloop commanded by the pirate Benjamin Hornigold.

1716 Captain Benjamin Hornigold, Mentor.
Hornigold may have appointed Teach to command a vessel.

1717 (July 5) Blackbeard First Appears in Print.
The deposition of Mathew Musson recounts the wreck of his ship and how he met Captain Walker, who warned him of a New Providence settlement of pirates, including Teach.

1717 (Summer) Blackbeard and Stede Bonnet.
Blackbeard encountered the pirate sloop *Revenge*, commanded by Stede Bonnet, "The Gentleman Pirate." Bonnet had been an educated, wealthy landowner in Barbados before turning to piracy. Blackbeard invited Bonnet to sail with him but soon realized Bonnet was a poor leader and sailor. Blackbeard appointed one of his crew, Lieutenant Richards, to command *Revenge*, making Bonnet a prisoner aboard his own vessel.

1717 (November 4) More Notoriety for Blackbeard.
The *Boston News-Letter* reported that an English ship had been attacked by Teach, and that he had formerly sailed as a ship's mate from the port of Philadelphia.

1717 (Fall) Blackbeard in the Chesapeake.
The *Boston News-Letter* reported sightings of Blackbeard in and around the Delaware and Chesapeake Bays with Hornigold and Bonnet. The pirates headed for the Caribbean in the late fall.

1717 (November) The *Concorde* Is Attacked.
Only 100 miles east of Martinique, the French ship *Concorde* encountered Blackbeard and his company. The pirates were aboard two sloops, one with 120 men and twelve cannon, and the other with 30 men and eight cannon. The French vessel had lost 16 men crossing the Atlantic, and 36 others were seriously ill from scurvy and dysentery. They were powerless to resist the attack. The pirates fired only two volleys at *Concorde* before she surrendered.

The pirates took *Concorde* to the island of Bequia in the Grenadines, where the French crew and the enslaved Africans were put ashore. They seized the valuables. A cabin boy and three French crewmen voluntarily joined the pirates. Ten others were taken by force, including a pilot, three surgeons, two carpenters, two sailors, and the cook. Blackbeard left Bequia aboard *Concorde*, now renamed *Queen Anne's Revenge*, newly outfitted with additional cannon.

1717 (November) Captain Hornigold Retires.
A short time after the taking of the *Concorde*, Benjamin Hornigold accepted the King's pardon and retired from piracy.

1717 (December) Blackbeard Is Described.
Blackbeard sailed along the Lesser Antilles plundering ships, and by December he had arrived off the eastern end of Puerto Rico. Along the way, he took a number of prizes, including the sloop *Margaret*, captained by Henry Bostock. Bostock's later deposition provides the only eyewitness description of the pirate captain, revealing that he was "...a tall Spare Man with a very black beard which he wore very long."

1718 (April 4-5) Blackbeard Captures *Adventure*.
In the Turneffe Islands in the Gulf of Honduras, Blackbeard captured *Adventure*, and the sloop's captain, David Herriot, joined Blackbeard's crew. Blackbeard also captured the sloop *Land of Promise* and the prized large merchant ship *Protestant Caesar*.

1718 (late April) Blackbeard Captures a Spanish Sloop.
The pirates passed near the Cayman Islands and off Cuba captured a Spanish sloop, which Blackbeard added to his flotilla. He sailed back to the Bahamas for a few days and then northward up the American coast in the spring of 1718. At this point, Blackbeard's flotilla was made up of more than 300 pirate crewmen on four vessels: the flagship *Queen Anne's Revenge*, *Adventure*, *Revenge*, and his new Spanish prize.

1718 (May) The Blockade of Charleston, South Carolina.
Blackbeard blockaded the port of Charleston for nearly a week. The pirates seized several ships attempting to enter or leave the port and captured the crew and passengers. As ransom for the hostages, Blackbeard demanded a chest of medicines. The medicines were eventually delivered, the captives were released, and the pirates continued their journey up the coast.

1718 (c. June 10) *Queen Anne's Revenge* Is Run Aground.
One week later off North Carolina, *Queen Anne's Revenge* attempted to follow the smaller sloops in Blackbeard's flotilla into Old Topsail Inlet, now known as Beaufort Inlet. Eyewitness accounts, including the deposition of *Adventure's* former captain, David Herriot, claimed that Blackbeard intentionally grounded *Queen Anne's Revenge* in order to break up the company. The sloop *Adventure* was lost while trying to assist the stranded flagship. Blackbeard marooned 17 pirates on a deserted sandbar, stripped the flotilla of their provisions and plunder, and left Beaufort Inlet with a hand-picked crew aboard the Spanish sloop. Blackbeard renamed this sloop *Adventure*. Bonnet rescued the marooned men and resumed "apyrating" aboard *Revenge*, which he renamed *Royal James*.

1718 (October) The Death of Stede Bonnet.
Bonnet and his crew were captured near present-day Wilmington, North Carolina, and taken to Charleston, where they were tried for piracy. Most were found guilty and were hanged that November 8th. Bonnet escaped briefly but was recaptured and hanged on December 10, 1718.

1718 (November 22) The Death of Blackbeard.
Blackbeard accepted the King's pardon in Bath, North Carolina after grounding *Queen Anne's Revenge*. He married. By September 1718 he was back to his pirating ways. He sailed into Ocracoke Inlet unaware that Virginia Governor Alexander Spotswood was tracking his movement and had sent two Royal Navy sloops led by Lieutenant Robert Maynard. In a short, intense battle aboard Maynard's sloop, Blackbeard and a number of his fellow pirates were surprised, attacked, and killed when Maynard and his crew rushed the deck from below. Maynard returned to Virginia on *Adventure* with the surviving pirates. The grim trophy of Blackbeard's severed head hung from the sloop's bowsprit.

For Dea Jackson, designer extraordinaire
—J.P.L.

ABOUT THE ILLUSTRATIONS

Illustrations in this book are artists' interpretations of Blackbeard dating from just six years after his death to the present.
Blackbeard lived long before the invention of photography, and none of these artists ever met him.
They used stories, myths, documents, and their own imaginations to create likenesses of Blackbeard and his adventures.

Cover: Art © Don Maitz; Page 1: Public Domain; 2: Art © Don Maitz; 3: Public Domain; 4–5: "Duel on the Beach" by N. C. Wyeth; 6: © AAAC/Topham/The Image Works; 8–9: © 2005 by Gary Kelley; 10: © Bettmann/Corbis; 12–13: © Rick Farrell; 15: © Mary Evans Picture Library/The Image Works; 16: By permission of the Frank E. Schoonover Fund, Inc.; 17: BP America Inc.; 18–19: By permission of the Frank E. Schoonover Fund, Inc.; 20: By permission of the Frank E. Schoonover Fund, Inc.; 22–23: Illustration by Richard Schlecht; 24: © Rick Reeves; 26: © Bettmann/Corbis; 27: © Bettmann/Corbis; 28: Erich Lessing/Art Resource, NY; 29: From *The Pirates Own Book*/Marine Research Society, 1837; 32: © Gary Kelley.

BIBLIOGRAPHY AND RESOURCES

Butler, Lindley S., *Pirates, Privateers and Rebel Raiders of the Carolina Coast*, University of North Carolina Press, Chapel Hill, N.C., 2000.
Hughson, Shirley Carter, *Blackbeard & The Carolina Pirates*, Port Hampton Press, Hampton, Va., 1894, 2000.
Lee, Robert E., *Blackbeard the Pirate: A Reappraisal of His Life and Times*, John F. Blair Publishers, Winston-Salem, N.C., 1974.
Moore, David, "Blackbeard the Pirate: Historical Background and the Beaufort Inlet Shipwrecks," *Tributaries*, Number 7, October 1997.
Moore, David, "Blackbeard's Capture of the Nantaise Slave Ship *La Concorde*: A Brief Analysis of the Documentary Evidence," *Tributaries*, Number 11, October 2001.
Shomette, Donald G., *Pirates of the Chesapeake: Being a True History of the Pirates, Picaroons, and Raiders on Chesapeake Bay, 1610-1807*, Tidewater Publishers, Centreville, Md., 1985.
Johnson, Captain Charles, *A General History of of the Pyrates*, T. Warner, London, England, 1724.
Johnson, Captain Charles, *A General History of the Lives of the Most Famous Highwaymen, Murderers, Street-Robbers, Etc.*, Olive & Payne, 1736
www.nationalgeographic.com/pirates/bbeard.html
www.imacdigest.com/blackbrd.html ("Blackbeard's Shipwreck" by David Moore)
www.unmuseum.org/pirate.htm (The Golden Age of Piracy)
www.ocracoke-nc.com/blackbeard
www.qaronline.com
www.blackbeardlives.com
www.legends.dm.net/pirates/blackbeard.html (Legends, Pirates and Privateers)
www.thehistorynet.com/HistoricTraveler/articles/1997/1097_text.htm (In Search of Blackbeard)

Text for this book is set in 1722 from P22. Display text is set in Roanoake, also from P22.

LIBRARY OF CONGRESS CATALOGING-IN-PUBLICATION DATA
Lewis, J. Patrick.
Blackbeard, the pirate king / by J. Patrick Lewis.
p. cm.
ISBN 10: 0-7922-5585-2 (hardcover) — ISBN 10: 0-7922-5586-0 (library binding) / ISBN 13: 978-0-7922-5585-7 (hardcover) — ISBN 13: 978-0-7922-5586-4 (library binding)
1. Teach, Edward, d. 1718–Juvenile literature. 2. Pirates–Biography–Juvenile literature. I. Title.
G537.T4L49 2006   811'.54--dc22   2005029514

One of the world's largest nonprofit scientific and educational organizations, the National Geographic Society was founded in 1888 "for the increase and diffusion of geographic knowledge." Fulfilling this mission, the Society educates and inspires millions every day through its magazines, books, television programs, videos, maps and atlases, research grants, the National Geographic Bee, teacher workshops, and innovative classroom materials. The Society is supported through membership dues, charitable gifts, and income from the sale of its educational products. This support is vital to National Geographic's mission to increase global understanding and promote conservation of our planet through exploration, research, and education.

NATIONAL GEOGRAPHIC SOCIETY
1145 17th Street N.W. · Washington, D.C. 20036-4688 · U.S.A.
Visit the Society's Web site: www.nationalgeographic.com
Printed in the United States of America

For information about special discounts for bulk purchases, please contact National Geographic Books Special Sales: ngspecsales@ngs.org.